Basingstoke
in old picture postcards volume 2

by Robert Brown

European Library ZALTBOMMEL/THE NETHERLANDS

Cover picture:
Original postcard for the cover of
this book.
'Sigillum co'e ville de Basingstoke'
means 'small images assembled of
places in Basingstoke'.

BACK IN TIME

GB ISBN 90 288 6451 2

© 1997 European Library – Zaltbommel/The Netherlands

Introduction

This second volume of 'Basingstoke in old picture postcards' brings together another selection of photographs of this Hampshire town during the Victorian age and through to the 1930's.

When Queen Victoria came to the throne in 1837 Basingstoke was on the verge of a commercial and industrial revolution. Within two years the railway had arrived in the town, and this, in turn, led to the expansion of certain local businesses, with the realisation that goods could be transported further afield than ever before. One such firm was Wallis and Haslam, who opened up in Station Hill to make agricultural machines, and within forty years had expanded its workshops from the top of the hill to the bottom. Later on the firm changed its name to Wallis and Steevens and became world famous for its road rollers. Another local firm which was to become popular for its products was Thomas Burberry's. Their raincoats were so well known that even Royalty began to wear them, and soon the factory, that was set up in Hackwood Road, was producing hundreds of them. In Church Street Alfred Milward opened a shoe shop, which later became a symbol of good quality footwear, and within a few years he had established similar shops all over the country. By the end of the 19th century other firms had broken away from the confines of local trade and were selling their goods internationally.

In 1898 the motor manufacturing firm of Thornycrofts moved into Basingstoke and started one of the largest industrial businesses in northern Hampshire. Once again the original small workshops that were built in Worting Road were to be extended and enlarged into roomy factory buildings. During the Great War and the Second World War the firm produced large quantities of machines and weapons with which to fight the enemy in Europe.

Meanwhile, with the advancement of local businesses bringing in more people to the town, the local council realised that certain amenities were lacking in the area. One of these was medical facilities, especially in the form of a hospital for all those people suffering from industrial accidents, and illnesses. The matter was dealt with by donations from various people and firms to build a cottage hospital on the corner of Hackwood Road and Southern Road, which was opened in 1879. Another essential service to the public was the need to educate the increasing number of children, so various schools were opened up across the town. Eventually they were all moved to the large Fairfields buildings after the Board Schools were established around the country. Adult education also became an important matter, and this was overcome by the opening of the Mechanic's Institute in New Street, where 'penny lectures' were held.

During the Victorian years Basingstoke's position as a market town became more profound with the construction of a Corn Exchange in Wote Street, then, later on, the opening of a cattle market next to the Railway Station brought even more trade into the town. Coupled with the weekly market in front of the Town Hall more and more shops opened up in the town centre, as well as banks and various offices. By the time that the 20th century had arrived Basingstoke was an important shopping place in Hampshire, and the arrival of the motor car brought more people from afar to partake in the many offerings that the local businesses sold. By the 1920's High Street stores such as Woolworth's, Boots the Chemists, and Timothy Whites and Taylors had opened up close to the Market Place.

The population increase by the turn of the century could not be contained by the private building of houses, as many people did not have the money to buy their homes. The natural increase by marriages and then childbirth brought about the construction of council houses in Cranbourne Lane, in 1914, then ten years later larger areas were acquired for housing estates, such as at Kingsclere Road and Grove Road. In the 1930's the South Ham Farm land was partly taken over for more housing.

By the early part of this century essential services, such as electricity, water, and gas, as well as sewers, had been installed in the town, while the emergency assistance of fire, ambulance and police vehicles were being organised. The fire station was built in Brook Street in 1913; the police station in Mark Lane, off London Street, in 1889; while an ambulance service was supplied by the St. John's Brigade. All this was to change in later years, especially after the Town Development Scheme of the 1960's, as locations were altered.

Religion was to play an important part in the progress of the town, especially in the late Victorian years, when the beliefs of the local folk varied between the Church of England and the smaller religious groups such as the Salvation Army and the Baptists. St. Michael's Church in Church Street was the main place of worship for the Church of England parishioners, having been built in the 16th century.

Communications in the form of the telephone, telegraphic, and postal services were set up in the town during the 19th century. The first telephone exchange was in an upper room above a shop in lower Wote Street, then later on a specially designed building was erected off New Street as more lines and equipment were needed. Next to the exchange was built a sorting office for mail, at the rear of the post office constructed in 1925, having moved from Wote Street.

Entertainment in the town varied from theatrical in the late 19th century, at the converted Corn Exchange, to cinematic at the three specially built cinemas in the early 20th century. Ballroom dancing at the drill hall in Sarum Hill in the Edwardian era was to be overtaken later on by more modern dancing in the 1930's. Sports clubs were opened up in the town as people found that they had more time for leisure, after the Great War, with more women taking part. This led to the long skirts of pre-war days being changed to the looser and shorter ones of the 1930's for easier movement when running and jumping. The Victorian way of life was soon to disappear.

In 1837 Queen Victoria was crowned – exactly one hundred years later King George VI was also crowned. In that century Basingstoke was to see drastic changes, especially in its population, which grew from 4,000 to 14,000. The size of the town was to slowly grow, especially in the 1930's, and the impending development of the 1960's was in the planning stages. The Second World War was to prevent any further housing or industrial growth in the town, but the past fifty years have seen expansion and alterations of a vast nature. Even now plans have been put forward for a new town to be built between Basingstoke and Winchester, at the village of Micheldever. The 21st century will evidently be a time for northern Hampshire to assess as to how much development it can absorb before it can say 'No' to the ever increasing housing estates being built across the once fertile agricultural land of southern England. Nature gave us the rolling hills of Hampshire to enjoy its green and pleasant land. Will we lose it all to gaze upon the bricks and concrete of an endless sea of buildings? It is up to us all to make that decision.

Acknowledgements

May I give my heartfelt thanks to the Willis Museum in Basingstoke in allowing me to reproduce some of their photographs of the town to complete this book. The majority of the pictures herewith are from my collection of old Basingstoke, assembled over the past 45 years, while the information has been obtained from a multitude of books, manuscripts, and documents from all over the country. My thanks also go out to all the hundreds of people who I have interviewed over those years, many of whom have given me valuable information on life in Basingstoke early this century.

Robert Brown

1 The Basingstoke Mote Hall, in the Market Place, which was there between 1657 and 1831. This lithograph was produced by Robert Cottle, who owned a shop in Winchester Street and was Mayor of Basingstoke five times. As well as a bookseller, printer, postmaster, councillor and church warden, he was also a donor of prize money for various causes. When he died in 1859 his business was acquired by Charles Jacob. The Mote Hall was replaced by a Town Hall in 1832 on the site of the three buildings on the right. The proprietors of the two shops and public house received a total amount of £3,636 as compensation for the demolition of their businesses and homes. The Town Hall is now the Willis Museum.

2 The Holy Ghost Chapel, in the Liten Burial Ground. This was one of many drawings and photographs produced in postcard form of the old building, which was previously the chapel of the Holy Ghost Guild in the 16th century. The building to the left was a schoolhouse. It was in the burial ground that the famous Mrs. Blunden was buried alive in 1674, after a hasty funeral. The wife of a malt merchant, she drank some poppy water by mistake, and went into a coma. The local 'doctor' thought she was dead, so she was immediately buried. Children from the school heard her calling out from her coffin, upon her wakening, and workmen dug her up, only to find she had died from her exertions to get out.

3 The Basingstoke Town Hall in 1841. This was another lithograph produced by Robert Cottle, who made several of the town's scenes. The Town Hall was built in 1832 at a cost of £10,000, with a small clock tower and an open lower frontage. This was enclosed in 1865, while a new and larger clock tower was erected in 1887. The Town Hall was used mainly as council offices until 1922, when the Municipal Buildings were opened in London Road. The interior of the Town Hall's ballroom, on the first floor, was decorated with several large paintings, purchased over a period of years. They were sold at Sotheby's in 1965.

4   The Vyne House at Sherborne St. John, a few miles north of Basingstoke. This Tudor mansion, with its famous lake, was built by Lord Sandys, and has been visited by Henry VIII and Elizabeth I. The house and land were the home of Sir Charles Chute until his death in 1956, when it was bequeathed to the National Trust. The Vyne House has an example of a classical portico and an impressive staircase. For the past two years a £2¹/₂ million restoration programme has been taking place throughout the building.

THE VYNE 1814

5 The Holy Ghost Chapel ruins and cemetery, with the Basingstoke railway station in the background. This lithograph was produced in 1841 by Robert Cottle, and later used in his Winchester Street shop for sale to customers. Also in the background is Mr. Whistler's windmill, which was built before the railway arrived. With the mill being cut off from the town by the Southern line, then later on by the Great Western line, coupled by the noise of the trains, Mr. Whistler closed his business down. He later sued the railway companies and received £905 compensation.

6 An old drawing of the Fleur-de-Lys Inn in London Street. Dating from the 16th century it was the resting place for Oliver Cromwell during the Civil War and the siege of Basing House. When the Marquis of Winchester was captured from his castle at Old Basing and placed into the cellar of the Bell Inn in London Street, Cromwell stayed at the Fleur-de-Lys for several nights. The inn was demolished in 1870 and a new building was built on the site, called Falcon House. Part of this still remains, being the shop to the left of the present post office.

7 Upper Wote Street in the 1870's, showing the Corn Exchange which was built in 1865. Between this building and the rear of the Town Hall was an opening where tradesmen sold meat, poultry, fish and vegetables. In 1884 this area was enclosed and called the Lesser Markets, which consisted of small shop units. In 1982 it was structurally altered for an extension to be built to the Haymarket Theatre, which the Corn Exchange later became. A drinking fountain which used to be at the rear of the Town Hall was fitted into the wall of the theatre in Wote Street.

8 An illustration of Basing House, at Old Basing, near Basingstoke, before the siege of 1642-1645. During the Civil War, when there were constant conflicts between Charles I and his opposition in Parliament, Basing House became the focus of Oliver Cromwell's army in a bid to oust the Marquis of Winchester and his friends. After a long stand-off the castle was taken in October 1645 and later destroyed by fire. The Marquis was held prisoner at the 'Bell Inn' in London Street, Basingstoke, then transported to the Tower of London.

9 The Three Tuns Inn, in Winchester Street, which is now the site of Parker's estate agents. This drinking house was demolished at the turn of this century, and the present building was erected. The gate on the left of the picture led into a yard which separated the inn from the butcher shop of George Lansley. In 1899 this yard and land stretching up to the Fairfields Schools were purchased by the local council for the construction of a new road, leading down from the road known as Back Lane but later called Southern Road. The new road was called Victoria Street, after the reigning Queen. (She died within a few months of it being opened, in January 1901.)

10 The Fairfields area in the early 1880's just before the land was used for the construction of the Board Schools. Originally the site for fairs and other functions, this was the scene of much development at that time, with several roads of private houses being built close by, including Beaconsfield Road and Jubilee Road, both being named in connection with the Victorian era. The land on the far left was used in 1915 to build the All Saint's Church. The Fairfields Schools were erected to house 1,300 children and opened in February 1888.

11 Fairfields School, in Council Road, which was built by a local building contractor, H. J. Goodall, in 1886. It was opened as a Board School on 16th February 1888 to house 1,300 children. The building in the picture was the Secondary School, while the Primary section was further down the road. The crowns on the roof, at each end of the building, were later removed, in 1939, to prevent them being blown down during any air raids in the Second World War. The bell tower, in the centre, was silenced when the rope hanging down broke, and it was never replaced.

Fairfields Schools Basingstoke.

12 Hackwood Road, looking north towards Southern Road and the London Road. Hackwood Road was once called Duke Street, as it led to Hackwood Park, the Duke of Bolton's estate. The white thatched cottage on the right belonged to the tollgate which existed in the 19th century. It was removed in 1861, while the cottage was demolished in 1929. In later years a house and shop were built on the site, called 'The Toll House Kiosk', which was kept by William Weaver, then it was taken over by Mr. J. H. Carter. Visitors to the War Memorial Park, the entrance to which was next to his shop, would buy confec-tionery and icecreams from there, especially during the annual carnival weeks.

13 The Cottage Hospital, on the corner of Hackwood Road and Southern Road, shortly after its erection in 1879. Costing some £2,000 to be built, it was enlarged in 1887, 1896, 1919 and 1955. In 1935 a 'New Hospital Building Scheme' was launched, and between 1936 and 1939 annual carnivals were held in the town to raise funds to build a new hospital in Cliddesden Road, but the outbreak of war in 1939 brought the scheme to an end. The money that was raised was spent on an outpatients' department being built in Southern Road in 1955. Upon the Basingstoke Hospital being constructed in Aldermaston Road in 1969 the Cottage Hospital was partly closed. It was demolished in 1993.

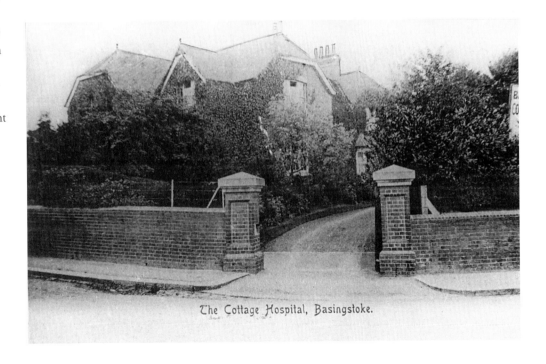

The Cottage Hospital, Basingstoke.

14 The Basingstoke Fire
Brigade early this century.
Formed in 1869, by 1878 it
had 24 members. The first
'station' was under the old
Wote Street Corn Exchange,
where the engine was kept.
Horses to pull it were in a
field near the railway station,
so much haste was made
whenever there was a fire. The
horses were ridden up to the
engine, hitched up, and then
driven off. This situation was
tolerated until 1913 when a
fire station was built in Brook
Street (at a cost of £1,100).
This station was demolished
in 1966, but by then a new
and larger one was built at
West Ham.

15 On 13th February 1914
Mr. William Buckland of Wote
Street, Basingstoke, was driv-
ing his car past the Dorchester
Arms Hotel at Hook, near
Basingstoke, when he was in
collision with a larger car
driven by Mr. Gilchrist of
Oakley Hall, Oakley, with the
result that Mr. Gilchrist was
killed instantly. A local photographer was on the scene
within a short time and took
this picture, which was later
made into a picture postcard.
In those days such a crash was
a major event, as there were
very few cars on the road.

Fatal Motor Accident at Hook. Feb: 13th 1914.

16 A faded postcard showing Winton Square, between Sarum Hill and Winchester Street, as it was in Edwardian days. Winton Square received its name from a large ladies' Boarding School called Winton House. The building was later used for offices for the telephone company, then for a computer firm. In January 1991 a fire badly damaged the building but it was soon repaired. The shop to the left of the picture was to change hands several times, and during the Second World War was the local Food Office. The water trough, a remnant of the Victorian days, was struck by a bus in the 1950's and removed.

17 Oakley village, with the pond to the right of the picture. After the Great War a number of smallholdings became established in the area, and soon an assembly of market growers, poultry farmers, and nurserymen made up a large percentage of the village population. The village, made up of East Oakley and Church Oakley, was originally centred around Rectory Road, Oakley Lane, and Hill Road, with the pond close by. The two main buildings were St. Leonard's Church and the National School. The latter, built in 1863, could not cope with the population increase of later years, so a new one was built for the extra children.

18 Worting village at the turn of this century, showing the narrow railway bridge on the Basingstoke to Andover road, which is known locally as 'The Tunnel', due to its length taking four lines of track – two to the West Country and the other two to Winchester and beyond. The house on the left was later altered into a shop called Habberfields, which sold groceries, while the tree by its side, used in the old custom of 'beating the bounds', was cut down in recent years. The house was also demolished to make way for a new road into Kempshott Lane and for the construction of several maisonettes.

19 London Street about 1900, when only the horse and cart stirred the dust of this main road through Basingstoke. Harry Powell's music shop, on the corner of May Place, next to the Congregational Church, was opened in 1856. In 1936 the building was taken over by Clarke's Piano House, which sold gramophones, records and musical instruments. Further along the road, on the left, the Red Lion Hotel was open for all travellers and visitors. Originally a two-storey building for stage-coaches to call in while journeying between London and the West Country, it has extended several times over the past years.

20 London Road looking eastwards from the town centre, at the turn of the century. Eastrop Lane is on the left, which used to lead down to the Basingstoke Canal bridge, while the old established 'White Hart' public house is on the right. Just past the inn was the garage of Tysoe and Cutler, established in 1918, which later became Tysoe and Lewin. In 1969 the old garage was demolished to be rebuilt in a more modern style. Many of the tall trees in London Road were planted by William Forder Smith, the Mayor, and Mr. Prestoe, of Wote Street, in 1869. Along the stretch of the London Road there used to be a toll-house and gate, but these were removed in 1867.

40238. BASINGSTOKE: LONDON ROAD.

21 Flaxfield Road (right) and Mortimer Lane at the turn of the century, when the corner was used as a dumping ground for waste produce. In October 1902 the local council opened a Town Yard in Basing Road at a cost of £3,000, for people to dispose of their rubbish. It was also used as a base for council vehicles. Flaxfield Road was once the dividing line between the Soke (lower) and Upland (upper) parts of Basingstoke. Local cricket matches were often held between people living in these areas.

22 Lower Church Street, showing part of St. Michael's Church, the parish church, which was mainly built in the 16th century. To the left, just past Mr. Purdue's general stores, is the entrance to Church Square, which led on to Mortimer Lane. The road was narrow at this point, hence the term 'Lane', but in later years it was widened. In more recent years it has again been given a narrow entrance, in a bid to ease the amount of traffic. Note the overhead street lighting, before lampposts were erected, and, in the distance, tall trees have a cluster of birds' nests – a common feature in the centre of the town in the Edwardian years.

Church St. Basingstoke.

23 The London and County Bank building in London Street at the turn of this century. The company had its head office in Lombard Street in London. Built in 1864, the building later became another bank, the Westminster, which in recent years became the National Westminster Bank. To the left of the picture was Mr. Cannon's butcher's shop, which is now the main post office.

24 The painted soldier at Mapledurwell Farm, nearly four miles east of Basingstoke. It was painted by Mr. Robert Clark, a member of the family who ran the farm for some three hundred years. Put on the side of the stable in the early 19th century, the painting originally showed the Grenadier Guard with sergeant's stripes and the rifle at an angle of 45 degrees (as in this photograph), but when it was repainted just before the Great War of 1914-1918 the stripes were left off and the rifle was placed at a horizontal position.

MAPLEDURWELL FARM.

25 Numbers 6 and 8 London Street – which was originally the Bell Inn. Dating back to the early 17th century this tavern was later extended into an inn to allow travellers to rest overnight. In 1645 the Marquis of Winchester was kept in the cellar after being captured by Oliver Cromwell at the end of the Basing House siege, during the English Civil War. The Marquis was then transported to the Tower of London the following day, and released some years later. The inn remained in business until the 1890's, then later became Boot's the Chemists in 1925.

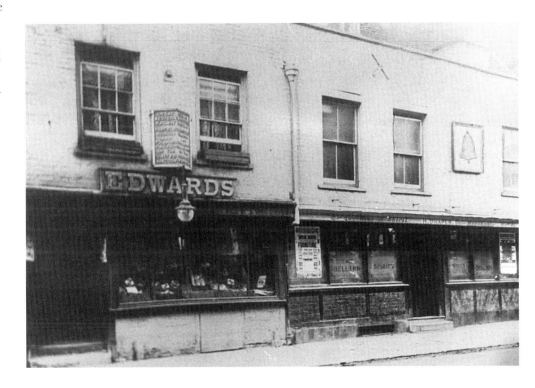

26 The construction of the Alton Light Railway in 1900. This line was built between Basingstoke and Alton at a cost of £67,000 and served the villages of Cliddesden, Herriard and Lasham, as well as other communities in that area. During the Great War the tracks were taken up in 1916 for use in France, then replaced in 1924. The railway was not a financial success, so in 1936 it was closed down, the last passenger train running in 1932. Before its closure two films were made on the line: 'Oh, Mr. Porter' (with Will Hay) and 'The Wrecker'.

27 Winchester Street in 1897 during celebrations for the Diamond Jubilee of Queen Victoria's accession to the throne, which took place in 1837. The structure on the far right of the picture was removed four years later for the construction of Victoria Street. The shop on the left, Wadmore's, was established in 1873 then sold to Mr. H. C. Ody in 1906, having survived the disastrous fire at Burberry's store the previous year. Burberry's (centre) sold a variety of goods for the home, and was the largest store in the town.

28 Upper Wote Street in the 1890's with the Corn Exchange on the right and the Town Hall in the background. The Corn Exchange, built in 1865, was in the process of being converted into a place of entertainment, as the cattle market, established in 1873 next to the railway station, had taken much of the trade away from the building. The 150 cattle stands inside the Corn Exchange were removed and a stage and other fittings were installed. Under the ownership of several people over the following years it became a roller-skating rink, a cinema and a theatre. In 1951 it became the present Hay-market Theatre.

29 The Wheatsheaf Inn at North Waltham, a village about five miles south-west of Basingstoke. The track seen in the picture was later to become the main road to Winchester and Southampton, when motorised traffic became the trend after the Great War. The A30 Ministry of Transport road branched off to Andover at this point and over the following years it became a very busy highway. It was widened and strengthened until the 1960's when the M3 motorway was constructed and opened a few miles away. The public house continues to flourish and is as popular now as it was a hundred years ago.

4015. "The Wheatsheaf" North Waltham.

30 The Great Western Railway station, which was in operation from 1848, when the line was opened between Basingstoke and Reading, until 1948 when the railways were nationalised. After this the building was used as a social club, but in more recent years it was demolished. This station used to face the Great Western Hotel, while the present main station, which used to be the Southern Railway station and was built in 1839, faces the new town centre.

31   John May, the local brewery owner and benefactor, opened the new cricket pavilion at Bounty Road, on 4th July 1901. He also announced that the Basingstoke Cricket Club would be renamed the Basingstoke and North Hants Cricket Club. The land had previously been purchased by John May for £1,800 in 1880, when the area was threatened to be sold for building plots. In 1900 the cricket ground was enlarged at John May's own expense, and in 1905 the ground was handed over to the trustees of 'May's Bounty', which the land subsequently became known as. John May died in 1920.

32 The Basingstoke Canal at Odiham. This was one of many places that the canal went through on its route from Basingstoke to the River Wey. Constructed between 1788 and 1794 the waterway was to bring trade in the way of exports of timber, flour and malt, and imports of coal, iron and oil. The canal was officially opened in 1796 having cost £190,000. The arrival of the railway in 1839 brought about a decline in the transport of goods resulting in the canal company being wound up in 1869. Various other companies acquired the canal in the following years, but by 1900 goods by canal to the Basingstoke wharf had ceased.

33 The Borough Police Force prior to the amalgamation with the County Police Force in 1889. The Borough police had their station in New Street, built in 1816, while the County police station was to the rear of the Grapes Hotel in Wote Street. Both stations closed upon the opening of the new Mark Lane Police Station to accommodate the new Police Force. The New Street station later became the home and business of Mr. Doman, the jobbing builder and decorator, who had set up his business in 1875. The cells under the police station remained there until the building was demolished some twenty years ago.

34 St. Michael's Church, in Church Street, the parish church of Basingstoke. Mainly built in the 16th century, further work was carried out in later years to prevent deterioration of the stone-work and timbers. During the 19th century the organ was replaced in 1866; the pinnacles were erected on the tower, 1879; and railings were fitted around the graveyard in 1817. In 1920 a War Memorial Chapel was built on the Church Street side, in memory of those who died during the Great War. In 1938 a serious fire in the roof of the church caused much damage; and in 1940 further devastation was brought about by three enemy bombs during the Second World War.

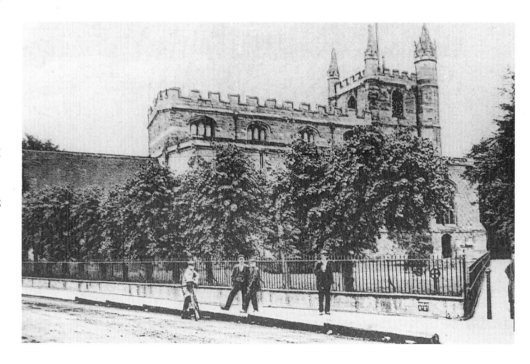

35 Sarum Hill, looking towards its junction with Flaxfield Road, before the houses were built on the field on the left, this being the Brambly Grange estate. In 1912 Penrith Road was built across part of the estate, from opposite Flaxfield Road, and, during trench digging for the houses, remains of a Mesolithic settlement were found. Items dating back to 5000 B.C. were discovered as workmen dug into an embankment. In 1939 Brambly Grange road was built, but upon the outbreak of the Second World War the last houses in the close were never completed.

36 Worting village, to the west of Basingstoke, showing the Old Forge in the centre of the picture. This small building was built in 1863 and was in continuous use until the 1970's, the last family in charge being the Trenchards. In the Victorian days there were two blacksmiths in the village. Other traders were a butcher, a tailor, a breeches maker, two grocers, and a shoemaker. There were two inns, the White Hart and The White Horse, although the latter was demolished and replaced by the present Royal Oak further along the road. The village also has many other features and buildings dating from olden days, including the church of St. Thomas of Canterbury, which was built in 1848 in a 14th-century style.

37 A very old faded photograph of the British School in Sarum Hill, which was built in 1841 at a cost of £650. This was one of several schools in the town. Later on, after the Board Schools were established in the 1880's, the British School was used by the Baptist Church and was officially opened as such in July 1908 with seating for eight hundred people. In 1994 the old building was demolished to make way for a Community Church.

38 Winchester Road in the late 19th century, with Brinklett's House on the right. The wall next to the house hid a farm-yard where an assortment of animals were kept, including a peacock. In the 1930's this yard was purchased to become Basingstoke's first car park, and later housed a Youth Club and various buildings for the Boy Scouts and other local youth organisations. These were demolished some fifty years later.

39 Winchester Street, with the entrance to Joice's Yard in the centre of the picture. The house on the left was later demolished to allow the National Provincial Bank to be built there. The square opening to its right was made into a shop unit, which in later years became the shoe shop of John Farmer Ltd. Above it the Prudential Assurance Company had its offices.

40 The lower section of Sarum Hill in Edwardian days, when the road was lined with trees, which was a common feature at that time. As road traffic increased over the following years, many of the trees were cut down. The houses on the left were demolished for the construction of the new Methodist Church in the 1960's. Several of the houses in Sarum Hill were used for businesses, one such place being at number 66, where Mr. William Grant ran a taxi. He began with one car in 1931 and continued single-handedly until 1957 when he retired. He died in 1965.

41 Brambly's Grange estate before the land was purchased for houses. Looking south towards Winchester Road, the path in the distance is still incorporated in the Bramblys Drive road that was built in 1939. The upper part was later called Bramblys Close, due to it being a cul-de-sac. The foreground of this photograph was part of Budd's Meadow, a field that stretched up to the Downsland estate. During the Second World War this meadow was used for growing sugar beet and other produce. Over the past thirty years the land has been used for private housing and extensions to the Technical College.

42 West Ham House, which existed to the west of the town off Worting Road. The grounds consisted of some 200 acres, part of which was used for farming. During the Great War a section of the gardens was used as a hospital for wounded soldiers. In the late 1940's Thornycrofts used the land for sporting purposes, and various functions were held there. In the early 1970's the land was slowly taken over for industrial and commercial use, and Grafton Way was built on the site of the old mansion.

43 One of several decorative postcards of Basingstoke produced in the early years of this century. The photograph shows the Town Hall, built in 1832, with its clock tower that was erected in 1887 and dismantled in 1961. The shop to the left of it was demolished for the construction of Lloyds Bank in 1923. The old Tudor style building behind it was incorporated into Lloyds Bank in 1962. The Basingstoke crest, on the right, depicts the English patron saint of St. Michael with the dragon, the feast day of which was celebrated with festivities on 29th September every year.

Town Hall and Market Place, Basingstoke.

BASINGSTOKE

44 Viables crossing, this being the point where the Alton Light Railway crossed the Harrow Way track before the construction of the Basingstoke by-pass in 1931. The railway was built in 1901 for passengers and goods to travel from Basingstoke to Alton and back. During the Great War the track was taken up to be used in France for the troops, then returned ten years later. The railway closed down in 1936. In the background (right) is Viables Farm, which is now used for a Crafts Centre.

45　An Edwardian postcard of the Market Place looking towards Winchester Street. The Old Angel Café on the left was in the building which was once the Angel Inn, an old coaching inn that dated back to the 16th century. The inn closed down in 1866 and remained empty for some time, then the archway into the rear of the building was sealed up and the old inn was transformed into shops and a café. Much of the inn was pulled down in 1915 and during the late 1920's. In later years the site was used by the International Stores and Barclays Bank.

46 Moose Hall in upper Church Street. Built for the Baptist Church in 1867 it later became one of the local halls for meetings, dances, wedding receptions and other activities. Next door to the bakery of Mr. Brickell, Moose Hall was saved from a severe fire in 1927 when the bakery and shop were gutted. It was hoped that the hall would be saved from demolition during the building of the new shopping centre in the 1960's, but in July 1979 it too was pulled down.

47   Winchester Street during preparations to celebrate the Coronation of King George V in 1911. To the left was Milwards shoe shop which was established in Basingstoke in 1857, in Church Street, by Alfred Milward. Later on he moved to Winchester Street, having opened up branches all over the country. In 1970 the local shop was moved to the new shopping centre, where it remained until acquired by Clarks Shoes in 1996. The small building and adjoining premises in the centre of the picture were demolished in the mid-1930's for the construction of new shops, including Montague Burton's and James Walker's.

Coronation Day. Basingstoke, Winchester St.

48 The Sarum Hill Drill Hall, built in 1883 at a cost of £3,000 at the expense of Lt. Col. John May, for the local Volunteer Corps. The building was a structure of brick and corrugated iron, with a total depth of 100 feet and a width of 50 feet. Built basically for military purposes, with an armoury inside, it was also designed for public entertainment with a stage, fittings and dressing rooms at one end of the hall. Attached to the building was a masonic hall, which was built in 1885. In later years it became the Plaza Cinema, after being converted into a dance hall in 1925. The cinema closed down in 1954, then was taken over as a furniture store by the local Co-operative Society. In 1981 the building was demolished to make way for a large office block.

49   Kingsclere Road before the council estate was built in the 1920's. The two cottages on the left belonged to Merton Farm, which used to exist off Aldermaston Road before the land was acquired for town development purposes. The cottages are still there and are now used as a shop and residence. In the distance is the Roman Catholic Church which was built in 1902 in Sherborne Road and was dedicated to the Holy Ghost. On the right of the picture Percy Fisher established his leather works in 1913, having moved from London where he began the business in 1890. He died in 1921, but the factory continued until 1967 when it closed down.

50 Winchester Road at the beginning of the century, with the entrance to Brambly's Grange house on the left. This was the home of Lady Colquhoun until the Thornycroft family took it over at the turn of this century. In 1938 the land between Penrith Road (built in 1911) and Winchester Road was used for the construction of Brambly's Grange road with semi-detached houses. The cottage on the right of the picture was once the public house 'The Black Horse'.

WINCHESTER ROAD, BASINGSTOKE

51   One of many postcards made of the Market Place, this one being taken around 1910, showing the London Street side. The ornamental lamp-post was erected in memory of the May family, whose association with Basingstoke dated back for centuries, especially in connection with the brewery in Brook Street. The lamp-post was unveiled by the local member of Parliament, the Right Honourable Arther Jeffreys, on 1st October 1903. Of the shops in the background the fishmongers, Colebrook and company Ltd., were to remain in the area right through to the 1960's. The large corner shop was to become Timothy Whites and Taylors in later years.

52   New Street junction with Winchester Street in the Edwardian days. This was known in the early Victorian years as Stew Lane but, on being paved and widened to allow traffic to be diverted to the lower part of the town, it was called New Street. Unfortunately this caused problems with the postal services, as some mail went to New Road on occasions. Mr. Alfred Course's drapery shop was originally in Winchester Road before moving to New Street. In 1922 he again moved his business to Andover, where he died in March 1947.

53 Mr. J. Boyer and Sons' drapery shop in London Street. Established in 1880, the business was transferred to his sons after his death in 1912. When casual-wear became the fashion in the 1930's the business in outfitting began to decline, and in 1935 the shop closed down. Curry's electrical store took over the building, having moved from Church Street where they opened, in 1927, mainly as a cycle shop. The new shop supplied various electrical goods, toys, cycles and prams. Upon the new shopping centre being built in the lower part of the town Curry's moved to one of the malls in 1971.

54 Mr. George Lansley's butcher's shop on the corner of Winchester Street and Victoria Street, which was established in 1837. Later on the shop was enlarged to sell raw meat, groceries and cooked meat, as well as having a slaughterhouse at the rear. At Christmas-time work began at 4.30 a.m. and went on until 9 p.m., while the outside of the shop was dressed with turkeys, geese and other poultry. It remained in the family through to 1958 when the shop closed down. The building was demolished in 1962 to make way for new premises to be built. The last proprietor of the shop, John Lansley, died aged 90 last year.

55 The Worting Road about 1920, showing Thornycroft's factory site on the left and the cemetery on the right. The cemetery land was acquired after the Southview Liten burial ground reached its maximum capacity in 1906. The cemetery was opened and dedicated in May 1913, the 25 acre site costing nearly £3,000 to be laid out, including a lodge and small chapel. Thornycroft's land was acquired in 1995 for the construction of Safeway's store. The factory canteen (in the background on the right) was demolished early in 1997 to allow houses to be built on the land. At about the same time an extension was laid out to the cemetery, at the rear of the houses.

56 George Ayres, a well-known local gipsy, who 'haunted' the vicinity for many years at the turn of this century. Born in 1853 he was to become a loner, and he wandered around the district in his latter years acquiring work at various places to pay for his food and clothes. His fame brought about this photograph being taken of him, and he became quite a personality through his cheery banter. Unfortunately he was placed into the Park Prewett Mental Home, near Basingstoke, in 1922, and is assumed to have died there.

57 London Street, looking east from the Market Place, about 1920. This was at a time when the motor car was just becoming a popular form of transport, as can be seen by the two garages on the right. The 1920's was to see the arrival of Boots the Chemists (left) and Woolworth's store (right), which were to take over the small local shops in the foreground.

London Street, Basingstoke.

58 John Mares' clothing factory coach outing in the 1920's, with the factory in the background. Situated in New Street, the business was established in Basingstoke in the late 19th century for the making of various clothes, including their own make of raincoat, called the 'Peltinvain'. In 1896 the factory was extended, but in the following year a serious fire caused £7,000 worth of damage. Mr. Mares died in April 1930 but the business continued until the late 1950's. In 1964 the building was demolished to make way for the present entrance into Joice's Yard.

59 Cliddesden Road, near its junction with Hackwood Road, before these seven cottages were demolished in the 1930's. The site is now the Lamb Inn car park. Cliddesden Road was a direct route to the village of Cliddesden in those days, but since the construction of the M3 motorway, in 1970, traffic has to travel via Hackwood Road. Another obstruction is the Ring Road, southern section, which cuts across the Cliddesden Road near the Shrubbery House site.

60 Inside the workshop at Gerrish, Ames and Simpkins, the clothing factory at Station Hill. Known as the Carlington Works, the firm was established in 1878 and continued to produce clothing for various countries until the compulsory purchase of the site in 1966 for the Town Development Scheme. Clothes were exported to markets all over the world, including Columbia and Spitzbergen, the latter being a group of islands in the Arctic Ocean who bought jackets from the firm. During the Great War of 1914-1918 six thousand overcoats were sent to Constantinople, and after the 1923 earthquake in Japan a large order of woollens was sent to Yokohama city.

61 London Street during the period of the Great War, with the Congregational Church, built in 1800, on the right. This church originated from the Independent Chapel of earlier years, which was in Cross Street. The Congregational Church was lit by gas in 1837, enlarged in 1860, and given a Church Hall in May Place in 1907. In 1972 the church came under the title of United Reformed, when the Presbyterian Church merged with them. During the demolition and rebuilding of the rear of the church in 1995 many interesting discoveries were made.

62 Some of the hundreds of local people who gathered at West Ham estate in July 1919 to see the celebrations of Peace Day, which consisted of a variety of activities and entertainment to celebrate the end of the Great War of 1914-1918 the previous year. In the following years West Ham was the venue for many sporting occasions as well as other presentations, due to the motor firm of Thorny-crofts acquiring the land.

63 On June 19th 1915 the thatched public house 'Old House at Home' was the victim of a serious fire, which gutted the building. Owned by the John May Brewery (of Brook Street, Basingstoke) it was one of six public houses in the Bunnian Place area. It was rebuilt with a slate roof and remained there until the Town Development Scheme led to its demolition in 1968.

64 London Street from the New Road – Hackwood Road – London Road crossroads. The tall white building on the right is the old established Red Lion Hotel, a well-known coaching inn of the 18th century. In recent years it has been extended and enlarged. The buildings on the right were demolished for offices to be built, one of these being the 17th century Chequers Inn, which later became the Anchor Inn. During its demolition in April 1985 two medieval roofs were found, and these were retained in the new building.

65 The London Road garage and filling station at Basing, near Basingstoke, in the early 1920's. In 1927 the land nearby was purchased by Mr. C. J. Brake of Fleet, and he sold it off in plots at various prices. The land, in a triangle between London Road, Park Lane and Hatch Lane, eventually became an estate of bungalows and houses, 80 per cent of them being self-built. This estate became known as the Byfleet Manor Estate, and increased the population of the village of Old Basing by nearly 400, the 1921 population being 1,223. By 1931 it had risen to 1,641.

66   Part of the large timber yard that belonged to Mr. E. C. White in lower Wote Street. Mr. Edwin White's business was originally established in 1792, when the Basingstoke Canal was built. The wharf area was constantly used for loading up timber for transport to London. Sawmills were in action throughout the year and stacks of wood, cut into all shapes, were kept in large enclosed sheds. In December 1890 a devastating fire destroyed much of the yard, resulting in some £2,000 worth of damage. Prior to the old wharf being demolished in 1946, the business was sold to and amalgamated with the Basingstoke Timber Company in Brook Street.

67   Construction begins on the council estate between Kingsclere Road and Sherborne Road in the early 1920's. 63 houses were built in the first phase at a cost of £65,122, while the sewers and roads cost an extra £5,899. This was the first council estate to be built in Basingstoke, but over the following ten years other estates were planned for South Ham and the Grove Road areas. This particular block of houses was erected opposite the Roman Catholic Church in Sherborne Road.

68 The London Road, where it met the Basingstoke by-pass. The Common was on the left of the picture, which stretched up to the War Memorial Park. The cottage on the right was demolished in the late 1960's, when the area was drastically altered for the Town Development Scheme, which involved a roundabout and new road changes in connection with the nearby M3 motorway. More recently, the land on the right is being built on, as a housing estate.

69 New Street, close to its junction with Flaxfield Road and Cross Street. The old delapidated building shrouded by the tree was removed in 1923 to allow the road to be widened. Some years later this corner was acquired to build a row of shops, which were completed in 1934 and called Queen's Parade. The houses facing New Street, in Cross Street, also became shops, then in 1937 were acquired for the Southern Counties branch office of the National Farmers' Union Mutual Insurance Society. They remained there until 1970 when they had to move to a new building to allow Timberlake Road to be built. Recently the N.F.U. moved to Victoria Street into larger premises.

70   London Street, looking west towards the Market Place, about 1930. On the right were an assortment of shops from Boots the Chemists, which opened in 1925, to the small bakers shop and café known as the Devon Café, which was opened in the same year. Opposite was Woolworth's store, which opened in 1921. Next to Woolworth's was the drapery shop of Mr. Boyer, which was established in 1882.

71 Inside the Venture bus depot in Victoria Street in the 1930's. The Venture bus service was established in 1926 with one small bus, which clocked up 150 miles per week in its travels around Basingstoke. Within ten years it had developed into a fleet of 31 vehicles, some of which used petrol propulsion while others used oil. Prior to the Second World War the fleet carried about 1,200,000 passengers each year, while a staff of 80 were employed to operate the service. The company was taken over by the Red and White Bus Company in 1945. The depot was demolished in 1962 to make way for a new road system.

72 The Market in the late 1920's, when the motor car was becoming a major feature on the roads, as can be seen by the policeman on the corner of Wote Street and London Street in a bid to prevent traffic accidents at this dangerous spot. Timothy Whites and Kingdon's stores were to be prominent in the square for another forty years, until they moved down to the new shopping centre in 1968-1970.

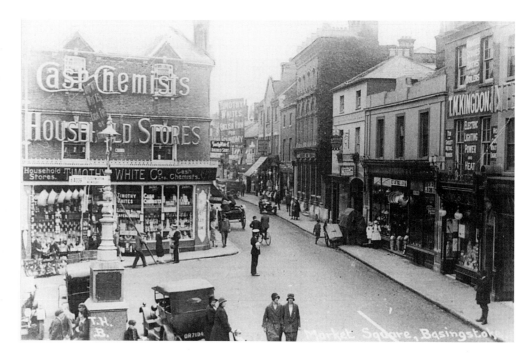

73 The North Lodge at Black Dam, known as the Keeper's Cottage. On the right is the old Harrow Way track, the line of which was used for the construction of the Basingstoke by-pass in 1931. In the background can be seen Ructstall Hill, now the site of a housing estate. The Black Dam land consisted mainly of thick reeds and muddy surrounds with four large ponds: Mill Head, Black Dam, Lower Fish Pond and Upper Fish Pond. There was an abundance of wildlife with swans, ducks, tadpoles and minnows. Plants such as meadowsweet and other wild flowers grew across the fields close to the ponds, while birds, some from the continent, made their nests in the mass of trees, hedges and grass.

74 An aerial photograph of Church Square showing St. Michael's Church on the left. In the 1930's the houses in the centre of the photograph were used as the residences and surgeries of two doctors and a dentist. In August 1940 these buildings, with others, were badly damaged by three bombs dropped by German aeroplanes during the Second World War. At least eight people were killed in the raid. The church was damaged, as was also the Methodist Church in Church Street.

75 The Plaza Cinema in Sarum Hill, decorated for the Silver Jubilee of King George V and Queen Mary in 1935. The Plaza, originally a drill hall built in 1883, was opened in April 1925 as the Pavilion Dance Hall, then, in October 1931 it was transformed into a cinema by Mr. George Casey, who also had the Grand Theatre and Cinema in Wote Street. Shortly after his Waldorf Cinema was built and opened in 1935 he died of pneumonia, so the three cinemas were run by his son-in-law, Mr. Christmas. The Plaza closed down in June 1954.

76 Merton Farm land, to the north of Basingstoke, with Sherborne Road leading to the village of Sherborne St. John on the right. This land now has the Aldermaston Road roundabout, and its various roads, on it, having been acquired for this purpose under the Town Development Scheme in the 1960's. Many other farms suffered the same fate, such as Buckskin, North Ham, Oakridge, Viables, South Ham, West Ham, Popley Fields and Chineham farms.

77 Wallis and Steevens' factory in Station Hill. This was part of the huge complex in which agricultural vehicles were made. In the early years of this century the firm became famous for their road rollers, which were used all over the world. Previously known as Wallis and Haslam the firm was established in 1860 in Station Hill, and over the years extended across to Reading Road and up to Clifton Terrace. In June 1967 the firm moved to the Daneshill industrial estate to allow the Town Development Scheme to evolve. A few years later Wallis and Steevens sold out to British Steel Piling. The business side moved to Ipswich while the agricultural section moved to Warminster.

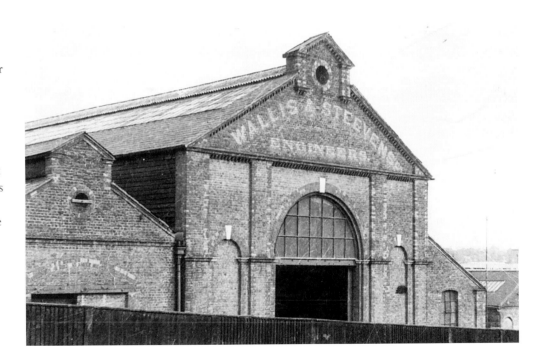

78 The Basingstoke Common before the alterations of the post-war years. In the background is the Ructstall Hill and Black Dam areas, where a multitude of wild life used to live before the housing estate was built there in the 1970's. During the Great War of 1914-1918 the Common was used as a huge army camp, from where the soldiers were sent to France. The original Common, 107 acres of it, was an integral part of the rural economy, for while the tenants worked the arable fields close by, they supplemented their livelihood by grazing their cattle on the common pasture.

79 The entrance to Carpenter's Yard, off Potter's Lane, between Wote Street and Church Street. Almost halfway along Potter's Lane this opening, with several cottages, led into a large area of land where various outhouses and other small buildings stood. Further down Bedford Place cut across the land, this being an alley-way with two rows of houses on either side, while below that was the greenhouses that belonged to Mr. Hedge's nursery. A legend states that Carpenter's Yard was used by smugglers to store their stolen goods en route from Southampton to London.

80 Sarum Place, a row of terraced houses in Sarum Hill, which were later demolished for the construction of the Trinity Church in the 1970's. In the interwar years these houses were the homes and businesses of several well-known people. Mr. Munford the decorator, Frank Hobbs the photographer, Mr. Rogers and Son the plumbers, and another plumber Mr. William Hall, were in this part of the road.

81 The Steam Dell repository, off Reading Road. In the interwar years the building was used for auctions, as well as for storage purposes. In the 1920's sales of poultry, eggs, wild rabbits, and farm and garden produce were sold there. Besides the weekly sales of agricultural goods there was also a monthly sale of other stock, such as harnesses and small vehicles, the auctioneers being Jennings and Lear, a local firm. Prior to them the auctions were held by Gillman, Sollom and Jennings. The repository was demolished in January 1988 to make way for offices to be built.

82 Eastrop Fields House off Eastrop Lane. This is a view from the rear of the building as the front was enclosed by trees. The home of Mrs. Simmons, J.P., in the interwar years, it had extensive gardens and grounds surrounded by tall trees on the Eastrop Lane side. On the Chequers Road side of the grounds were stables. In 1983 the house and grounds were cleared away for the construction of Geffreys Fields Old People's Home.

83 The old Assembly Rooms at the rear of the Angel Inn, in the Market Place, before its demolition in the 1960's. It was here that Jane Austen, the famous novelist (1775-1817) came to learn dancing, the upper floor being a well-known place for dancing lessons. In her early years Jane Austen lived at Steventon, a small village off the Andover road, where she began to write her stories about the upper middle class society of that time.

84 Brook Street Elementary School, which opened in 1909 with an average attendance of some two hundred children. The site of the school was previously two cottages, purchased by the Hampshire County Council for £565 in 1905. In 1930 an extension was built for the education of a further 180 children. When the Town Development Scheme of the 1960's led to a Ring Road being built through the school's large playground, the brick shelters were also demolished. In July 1985 the school closed down and its pupils were transferred to the Kings Furlong Primary School. Later on Brookvale School, as it later became known, was taken over by the Technical College.

85 Hackwood Park, a large private estate south of Basingstoke. The mansion was built in 1683 and completed within five years for Charles, 6th Marquess of Winchester. Elizabeth, Queen of the Belgians, spent most of the Great War years (1914-1918) at Hackwood Park. In 1935 Lord Camrose purchased Hackwood Park from Lord Bolton. Lord Camrose died in 1954, his son taking over the title until 1995, when he too passed away. The estate, consisting of large areas of trees, was badly hit by the storm of 1987 when masses of trees were blown down. Other features are the deer that roam the estate and the beautiful Spring Wood (80 acres). In May 1997 Lady Camrose died, leaving the estate to be sold.

86 Roman Road, near the railway bridge into Worting Road. The land on the right was later used for building private houses. To alleviate the traffic problem through the narrow bridge, this part of Roman Road was closed in 1971 and a diversion road was built to the west to enter Worting Road on the other side of the bridge. Roman Road was named after the original track that the Romans built around 50 A.D. during their conquest of Southern England, the Basingstoke section being part of the Silchester to Winchester road.

87 Winklebury House, a large mansion built close to Winklebury Camp, between the Kingsclere Road and Worting Road. The land belonging to the Bury Farm was cut up into small holdings in 1914, and rough tracks were laid to the various cottages that were built over the following years. In 1937 excavations were carried out in the area and items belonging to primitive days were found. From 1964 housing estates were built for the Town Development Scheme, and during this work a limestone coffin with a Roman skeleton was found at Winklebury. In 1971 Winklebury House was destroyed by fire after standing empty for several years.

88 Eastrop Church Hall, in Goat Lane. Built and opened in 1907 at a cost of £960 it became the meeting place for those attending the St. Mary's Church in Eastrop Lane. During the Second World War the hall was put at the disposal of the local Air Raid Precautions group. In the late 1960's the hall was demolished in conjunction with the erection of a new rectory and church hall. Eastrop was once a separate parish, divided by a long stone wall, part of which still remains. In the 1880's it was merged with the borough of Basingstoke.

89 The Nonconformist mortuary chapel at the Liten burial ground off Chapel Street. This was one of two such chapels built in 1858, the other belonging to the Church of England. Both chapels were built from the designs of Messrs. Poulton and Woodman of Reading, and each one had spires 80 feet high. They were officially opened on 1st July 1858, at the same time as the Liten burial ground was enlarged to form a public cemetery. The whole area once belonged to the Holy Ghost Guild, whose chapel was built in the 16th century, the ruins of which are still standing. The cemetery ceased to be used after the Worting Road cemetery was opened in 1913.

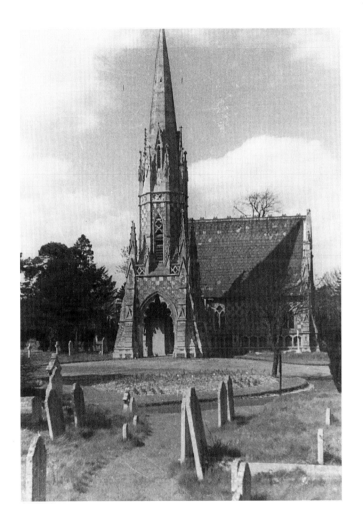

90 Merton Farm, off the Aldermaston Road, to the north of Basingstoke. The farm, owned by and named after Merton College, Oxford, had land extending over a large area, but over the years between 1920 and 1960 parts of it were purchased for residential and industrial purposes. At the turn of the century the farm grew the usual rotation crops, including wheat, barley, kale and beet, but the farm was best known for its herd of shorthorn pedigree cows, which produced an endless supply of milk for the dairy. The dairy closed in 1961 and the farm closed down in May 1967 for the Town Development Scheme.

91   Queen Mary's School in Worting Road. A Secondary School, governed by a scheme of the Board of Education, it was originally founded and endowed at the Liten, off Chapel Hill, in 1555 as the Holy Ghost School. Rebuilt in Worting Road in 1855, over the following years various schoolrooms and departments were added to the building. In 1939 the school was transferred to new buildings at the top of Vyne Road, and the Worting Road premises became a Technical College. In 1960 new college buildings were erected opposite, then in 1995 the old college (pictured here) was demolished and an entirely new and modern building was erected on the site, which was opened in October 1996 by Princess Anne.

92 Skippett's House, an early 19th-century country house, which was situated off the Basingstoke by-pass. The last owner, Mrs. Montagu, upon her wishes, was buried in the grounds of the house. The house was then acquired, in 1986, by Gould Electronics. Later on the house was demolished and the site was used for the construction of offices. It is thought that the original property on this twelve acre estate was a 17th century inn called 'The Skipper's'.

93 The offices and shop of the Basingstoke Timber Company in Brook Street. The timber-yard was on the left of the building. This old building was originally a mill, then in the 1880's it was used by the newly-arrived Salvation Army as a meeting hall. It became the target for roughs and toughs who despised the cries of 'ban all drink' and the Salvation Army's parades through the town, but eventually peace was restored and the religious group was accepted into the town. The building was demolished in 1967 for the Town Development Scheme, while the firm moved to the Daneshill Industrial Estate.

94 Loddon Lodge, off lower Wote Street, which was next to the Savoy Cinema. It became known as the 'Crooked House' due to it being undermined by the Loddon stream over a period of many years. Built about 1860 the house became the home of the proprietor of the Electric Cinema, which the Savoy was originally. In August 1966 the house was vacated and demolished a few months later for the new town centre.

95 Audley's Wood House, at Cliddesden, which dates from the mid-Victorian age. It was the home of the famous brewery family of Simmonds; and of William Bradshaw, who was the creator of the railway guides. In 1952 the property was bought by the Hampshire County Council, who adapted the building into an old people's home. The adjoining stable block was later converted into a work centre for the physically handicapped. The grounds are extensive and included in its original design was a sunken garden. In more recent years the house has been acquired as a hotel by the Thistle Group.

96   Buckskin Farm at Kempshott village, to the west of Basingstoke, which was farmed by Mr. Henry Gibbons between the two world wars. Buckskin Lane, originally a narrow country track, cuts across the scene to the Five-Ways junctions with Kempshott Lane and Pack Lane in the distance. It was here that steeple-chase races took place during the 18th and 19th centuries as people 'toed the line' along the course. The farm dates back to the 17th century, a plaque dated 1642 having been found in an outbuilding many years ago. The land belonged to Lord Camrose of Hackwood Park, until it was acquired in 1965 for the Town Development Scheme to build over a thousand homes.

97 St. Mary's Church at Old Basing village. This fine old church dates back to the 11th and 12th centuries, when the chancel and transepts were built. In 1664 the church was restored, but many of its original features were left, including the tombs of the Paulet family, who were associated with Basing House. During the Civil War, when Basing House was under siege, the Roundheads stabled their horses inside the church, and the walls of the building contain several bullet marks.

98 Kings Furlong avenue in the pre-war days. This tree-lined track led up to Kings Furlong house, off Winchester Road, but some years after the house was demolished in the 1950's, many of the trees were either blown down in storms or damaged by pipe-laying and cut down. The Kings Furlong estate now contains private houses and a school for Primary pupils.

99 Kempshott House, which stood near the present Basingstoke Golf Club at Kempshott. The mansion house dated from 1784, overlooking a large estate which is now the golf course. In 1795 the owner of the house, Mr. J. C. Crook, allowed the Prince of Wales and Caroline of Brunswick to use the house for their honeymoon. The royal romance broke down and when Prince George became King of England his wife was refused admission to Westminster Abbey. Their daughter, Charlotte, conceived at Kempshott House, died during childbirth at the age of 20 after marrying Prince Leopold of Coburg. Kempshott House was demolished during the construction of the M3 motorway in 1969, and only the old coach house remains.

100 The premises of Mr. Walter Lunn in Cross Street, who ran a wholesale confectionery business. He began the making of sweets for Mr. Buckland of Wote Street in 1926, then moved to Cross Street two years later. Over the following years the wholesale business was expanded to other shops and the premises were enlarged. Then in 1962 Mr. Lunn was informed that the site was needed for the Town Development Scheme and he closed down a few years later, the building being demolished in 1970.

101 Bunnian Place, an early Victorian street of terraced houses, which was to be demolished under the Town Development Scheme of the 1960's. Only one building remains – the Queen's Arms public house, which is one of some six drinking places that existed in that road at one time. This picture shows the west side of the road, with the foreground buildings being the offices of Smith Brothers, an old established firm of seed merchants, who sold a variety of other goods such as oilcake, manure, hay, corn and straw. Its close proximity to the Cattle Market allowed it to have a regular stream of customers on Wednesdays, when the market was held.

102 The Municipal Buildings, off London Road, before the alterations of post-war years, and the construction of the new Civic Offices, built in 1975. Originally a mansion house belonging to the Goldings estate, it was acquired in 1922 as the local council offices, after the land was purchased for a War Memorial Park the previous year. Goldings House was bought for £10,000 by the town council, who later, in June 1922, moved their offices from the Town Hall, in the Market Place, to the mansion.

103 Part of the old Basingstoke Workhouse in Basing Road, a large complex of buildings built in 1835 at a cost of £7,500. Besides having living quarters and other services for the poor, the Workhouse, located close to the railway, had a chapel as well. A master and a matron were appointed to look after the people in the building, most of whom were poor and had no home or money. Established after the Poor Law Act of 1835 the Workhouse was run by a Board of Guardians. In 1929 this board was abolished and the function of the buildings ceased. Many of those still there were given council homes, which had been built in the area at that time. The Workhouse was demolished in the 1960's and is now the site of the Hampshire Clinic.

104 South Ham farm before the Second World War. The trees on the right of the picture are those still standing in Peveral Walk on the South Ham housing estate. This agricultural land, which stretched from the Downsland area along the Andover road to Kempshott, was acquired over a period of fifty years for various phases of housing by the local council. The first encroachment was by the Alton Light Railway to lay their line from the main Southern Railway tracks to the town of Alton, some eleven miles away, in 1901. In the mid-1950's the actual farmhouse and outbuildings were demolished after the farm closed down.

105   Harvesting at Hatchwarren Farm, south of Basingstoke. Prior to the Second World War the gathering up of the harvest was carried out by hand with little help from machinery. The combine harvester, although invented as early as 1818, did not come into full operation in Britain until 1944. Hatchwarren Farm was run by Rex Patterson for many years until his death in 1978. The land was partly acquired for the construction of a large estate of houses in the 1970's, and even now further building is taken place across the original farm. Beside a vast amount of homes, the estate also has infant and junior schools, a community centre, a surgery, a thatched roofed public house, and a complex of shops, most of which have been built in the past few years.

106 Construction of the pharmaceutical firm of Eli Lilly off Kingsclere Road in 1938. Completed in March 1939 this British offshoot of the American company was built close to the main railway line. It was situated on the hill overlooking the town, painted white, and floodlit at night-time. The six-storey ferro-concrete building became a landmark, so-much-so that during the following Second World War it had to be covered in dirty brown and green camouflage paint in a bid to stop the German bombers seeing it as they flew over at night.

McAlpine's Contract at Basingstoke, 1938.

A28

107 An aerial picture of the Flaxfield Road and Essex Road junctions with Worting Road in pre-war days. Flaxfield Road (right) was known for the bakery owned by the Thornton family, who had shops and cafés in the town, the business being established in 1886. In 1957 a serious fire damaged the bakery, but the business continued for another ten years, when it closed down. The warehouse building in the upper part of the picture belonged to the Co-operative Stores, which was in Essex Road. The large yard was used for the annual Michaelmas Fair until the 1950's.

108 Miss Beryl Wiggins and her four Carnival attendants in 1938. The Basingstoke Carnival was established in 1937 to raise funds for the construction of a new hospital along Cliddesden Road, as the Cottage Hospital in Hackwood Road was becoming too small for the town's needs. It was intended to have the carnivals on an annual basis, but the outbreak of war in 1939 put an end to them, until they were re-introduced in 1956. The pre-war carnivals raised £3,400, which was used to build an outpatients' department in Southern Road, attached to the Cottage Hospital.